Blueprints
FOR MANAGERS

Compliments of

Joseph L. Brackner

The Blueprints Group, Inc.

Management & Leadership Skills Development

5806 Grove Avenue, Suite 100
Richmond, Virginia 23226

Direct: (804) 859-8250, Office: (804) 593-5900

THE ACHIEVERS

Written by Dr. Dan Leimann ♦ *Compiled by Kimberly Smithson*

Designed by Jenny Bumba

Great Quotations Publishing

THE ACHIEVERS written by Dr. Dan Leimann,
compiled by Kim Smithson
& book design by Jenny Bumba

ISBN: 1-56245-251-7

Table of C·O·N·T·E·N·T·S

A·C·H·I·E·V·E·R·S

PREFACE

What is it that Albert Einstein, Ralph Waldo Emerson, Abraham Lincoln, Alexander Graham Bell, Oprah Winfrey, Colin Powell, Michael Jordan, Walt Disney, Amelia Earhart and Ronald Reagan all have in common? While certainly all have become leaders in their fields, leadership alone does not create heroes or make legends. Achievement is what sets them apart.

Whether it's overcoming obstacles, beating the odds, incredible luck or simply dogged persistence, we tip our hats to those who have the ability to get things done — the innovators who fundamentally change the way the country is run, society functions or the game is played. Achievers are the doers, movers and shakers of society.

What common characteristics could E=Mc2 possibly share with a gravity — defying Air Jordan legend? A transatlantic flight have with the longest modern economic expansion? A military strategist have with a journalist? These leaders employ the common characteristics of achievers.

Whatever their field, achievers are *Action-oriented*. They get things done. They study, prepare, practice, focus, and execute with care and precision. Achievers do not wait for things to happen to them … they happen to things.

Communication is a skill that elevates achievers and makes them leaders. If Oprah Winfrey didn't have the ability to moderate the flow of communication between her guests and reduce complicated concepts into simple, easy-to-understand language, how popular would her show be? Would Ronald Reagan have been able to pass the necessary legislation to guide the country into economic prosperity had he not been able to communicate his vision to the people? Communication translates chaos into order. Those who can use the power of language have a tremendous advantage.

Throughout history *Honesty* has been revered. The concept of "a man's word is his bond" dates back thousands of years, and it is just as pertinent today. Integrity, truth, trust, and honesty are characteristics that society demands of its leaders. "Do what you say you are going to do when you say you are going to do it … " is sound advice to give to anyone in business, athletics, or life. *A leader has to be believed before he can achieve.*

Intuition is something that most people scorn as an airy concept. However, most achievers will admit that they have learned to trust their instincts. Successful athletes will speak of a **feel** for the game, investors take tremendous risks based on their **gut**, the best journalists use their intuition to explore a **story**, and the top salespeople use their sales-**instincts** to satisfy their customers.

Achievers are passionate about their work. *Enthusiasm* separates the winners from the losers. Those with average talent who throw their hearts into what they do will always finish at the top. Flaming enthusiasm backed up with horse sense is the formula for success.

Achievers are oftentimes *Visionary*. They possess the ability to clearly see results in the future, and how to get from here to there. Achievers are strategizers, planners, and leave very little to chance. It takes a visionary individual like Colin Powell to coordinate and plan a military operation with little loss of life. Abraham Lincoln was persistent in his vision to end slavery without jeopardizing the union of states, and Alexander Graham Bell had a vision of how to communicate with another without being face to face.

Sometimes the best laid plans go awry, and it takes *Extra-Effort* to make things happen. The history books are full of ancient and modern heroes who overcame adversity and won, despite the odds, through determination, perseverance and unrelenting energy. Many people give up just before they reach the summit of achievement, and for lack of a little extra effort, they fall into the nameless ranks of mediocrity. It is so true … there are no traffic jams on the extra mile. If you want to make a name for yourself, give a little more. Go above and beyond expectations.

The balance of being visionary and innovative must be tempered by being *Realistic*. There are people who get so absorbed in their dreams and fantasies, they fail to be realistic. They fail to set realistic goals. Walt Disney created a billion dollar business dealing in dreams and fantasy, but his enterprise would never have succeeded if he had not set realistic goals for achievement.

Few people can achieve and succeed without rendering *Service* to others. Making the wants and needs of others a priority, is the hallmark of true achievers. Whether it's serving customers, fans, a continuency, society, or simply those less fortunate, others recognize such selflessness and appreciate the effort. Customers reward a commitment to service with their patronage, their vote, or their referral, but sometimes the achievers' reward is simply the satisfaction within themselves that they made a positive difference.

By employing the characteristics of achievement; being Action-oriented, Communicating effectively, being Honest, using Intuition, being Enthusiastic, having the Vision to plan, putting forth the Extra-Effort necessary to win, being innovative yet Realistic, and rendering Service to others, an ***ACHIEVER*** results*!*

ACHIEVERS

ACTION

Achievers are action oriented:
They put the **GET IT DONE** into their plans. All of us have
dreams we hold in our hearts that we hope will come true one day.
Achievers make dreams actual goals. Each goal has a plan,
and each plan is acted upon. Unexpected barriers that
are encountered are overcome by effort and ingenuity and not
looked upon as excuses for defeat. Somehow they are able to
make and take the steps that bridge concept and reality.

They are able to take their **hopes** and shape them into an even
larger, more rewarding reality through effort.
Dreams without action to make them come true are merely
big ideas. Certainly, if a dream is worth thinking about,
it merits the effort to make it come true. All that is needed
is a plan and follow-through. Achievers attain success
through hard work, not luck, because they are eager to get on with
their work so that their ideas may become reality and so their
minds may once again be free to dream.

A·C·H·I·E·V·E·R·S

"A rolling stone gathers no moss."

— Publilius Syrus —

"It is better to be making the news than taking it; to be an actor rather than a critic."

— Winston Churchill —

"Man is not the creature of circumstances. Circumstances are the creatures of men."

— Benjamin Disraeli —

"That action is best which procures the greatest happiness for the greatest numbers."

— Francis Hutcheson —

"The will to do, the soul to dare."

— Sir Walter Scott —

A·C·H·I·E·V·E·R·S

"Things may come to those who wait, but only the things left by those who hustle."

— Abraham Lincoln —

"Strong convictions precede great actions.

— Unknown—

"Think like a man of action, act like a man of thought."

— Henri Bergson —

"Be not afraid of growing slowly, be afraid only of standing still."

— Chinese Proverb —

"There is something more important than believing: **ACTION!** The world is full of dreamers, there aren't enough who will move ahead and begin to take concrete steps to actualize their vision."

— W. Clement Stone —

A·C·H·I·E·V·E·R·S

"Don't be afraid to take a big step when one is indicated. You can't cross a chasm in two small jumps."
— David Lloyd George —
British Prime Minister

"The critical ingredient is getting off your butt and doing something. It's as simple as that. A lot of people have ideas, but there are few who decide to do something about them now. Not tomorrow. Not next week. But today. The true entrepreneur is a doer, not a dreamer."
— Nolan Bushell —

"Trust only movement. Life happens at the level of event not of words. Trust movement."
— Alfred Adler —

"The best actions are those which go above and beyond expectations."
— Kim Smithson —

"If there is a way to do it better … find it."
— Thomas Alva Edison —

A·C·H·I·E·V·E·R·S

"*Doing little things well is a step towards doing big things well.*"
— Anonymous —

"*Apply yourself. Get all the education you can, but then, by God, do something. Don't just stand there; make it happen.*"
— Lee Iococa —

"*You will learn and grow according to the nature and consequences of your actions.*"
— Robert Anthony —

"*Things do not happen; things are made to happen.*"
— John F. Kennedy —

"*Both tears and sweat are salty, but they render a different result. Tears will get you sympathy, sweat will get you change.*"
— Jesse Jackson —

A·C·H·I·E·V·E·R·S

"Do It! Let's Get Off Our Butts."
— *Book Title by John Roger and Peter McWilliams* —

"*People may doubt what you say but they will believe what you do.*"
— *Anonymous* —

"*You may have the loftiest goals, the highest ideals, the noblest dreams, but remember this, nothing works unless you do.*"
— *Nido Qubein* —

"*To know what has to be done, then do it, comprises the whole philosophy of practical life.*"
— *Sir William Osler* —

"*We learn by doing.*"
— *Aristotle* —

A·C·H·I·E·V·E·R·S

"Even if you're on the right track, you'll get run over if you just sit there."

— Will Rogers —

"Great ideas are a dime a dozen, and there's not a one that's worth any more without action."

— Anonymous —

"Wisdom is knowing what to do next, skill is knowing how to do it, and virtue is doing it."

— David Starr Jordan —

"You can't build a reputation on what you're going to do."

— Henry Ford —

"Professionalism is knowing how to do it, when to do it, and doing it."

— Frank Tyger —

A·C·H·I·E·V·E·R·S

"The distance doesn't matter; only the first step is difficult."
— Mme. du Deffand —

"We judge ourselves by our motives and others by their actions."
— Dwight Morrow —

"Learning is an active process. We learn by doing."
— George Bernard Shaw —

"Success is 1% inspiration and 99% perspiration."
— Anonymous —

"We are judged by what we finish, not by what we start."
— Anonymous —

A·C·H·I·E·V·E·R·S

The time for

action is now.

It's never too late

to do something.

— Carl Sandberg —

♦ ♦ ♦ ♦

Spend time putting

together the best

plan possible …

then do it …

drive it …

move it …

make it happen.

— Karyn Conway —

"*It is not so much how busy you are - but why you are busy. The bee is praised. The mosquito is swatted.*"
— Marie O'Connor —

"*As I grow older, I pay less attention to what men say. I just watch what they do.*"
— Andrew Carnegie —

"*Chaotic action is preferable to orderly inaction. Don't just stand there, do something.*"
— Karl Weick —

"*Thinking is easy, acting is difficult, and to put one's thoughts into action is the most difficult thing in the world.*"
— Johann Wolfgang von Goethe —

"*The reason a lot of people do not recognize opportunity is because it usually goes around looking like hard work.*"
— Thomas Alva Edison —

A·C·H·I·E·V·E·R·S

"Never mistake motion for action."
— *Ernest Hemingway* —

"If you put off everything till you're sure of it, you'll get
nothing done."
— *Norman Vincent Peale* —

"Indecision is often worse than wrong action."
— *Richard Nixon* —

"Take time to deliberate, but when the time for action has arrived,
stop thinking and go to it."
— *Napoleon Bonaparte* —

"Good purposes should be the director of good actions,
not the apology for bad."
— *Thomas Fuller* —

A·C·H·I·E·V·E·R·S

"The heights by great men reached and kept were not attained by sudden flight, but they, while their companions slept, were toiling upward in the night."
— *Henry Wadsworth Longfellow* —

"The great thing in this world is not so much where we are, but in what direction we are moving."
— *Oliver Wendell Holmes* —

"Do not be too timid and squeamish about your actions. All life is an experiment."
— *Ralph Waldo Emerson* —

"Success is a ladder that cannot be climbed with your hands in your pockets."
— *American Proverb* —

"I have always thought the actions of men the best interpreters of their thoughts."
— *John Locke* —

A·C·H·I·E·V·E·R·S

"Action is eloquence."
— William Shakespeare —

"Both tears and sweat are salty, but they render a different result.
Tears will give you sympathy, sweat will get you change."
— Jesse Jackson —

"I never knew a person who suffered from overwork. But there are
many who suffered from too much ambition and not
enough action."
— Dr. James Montague —

"Show me a man who cannot bother to do little things and I'll
show you a man who cannot be trusted to do big things."
— Lawrence D. Bell —

"A strategy needs to be driven into reality."
— Kim Smithson —

A·C·H·I·E·V·E·R·S

"*A constructive life is built of the things we do —
not of the things we don't do.*"
— Cavett Robert —

"*There is no try, there is either do or not do.*"
— Yoda, The Jedi teacher —

"*Our problem is not the lack of knowing; it is the lack of doing.
Most know far more than they think they do.*"
— Mark Hatfield —

"*A journey of a thousand leagues begins with a single step.*"
— Lao-tzu —

"*Acting on a good idea is better than just having a good idea.*"
— Robert Half —

A·C·H·I·E·V·E·R·S

"I know of no more encouraging fact than the unquestionable
ability of man to elevate his life by a conscious endeavor."
— Henry David Thoreau —

"Just do it!"

— NIKE® slogan —

"There are risks and costs to a program of action. But they are far
less than the long range risks of comfortable inaction."
— John F. Kennedy —

"Bite off more than you can chew, then chew it. Plan more than
you can do, then do it."
— Anonymous —

"Get action. Do things; be sane, don't fritter away your time …
take a place wherever you are and be somebody; get action."
— Theodore Roosevelt —

COMMUNICATION

Within the power of language lies the power of achievement. The ability to stir passions, to motivate action, and to initiate change is a common ability that achievers possess.

Whether it's a report, speech, letter, book, telephone conversation or a face to face meeting, an exchange of ideas takes place. Communication is a crucial component of our daily lives … at work or at home; in a professional setting or in an intimate relationship. For an idea to be clearly received, it has to be clearly sent.

Those who have the ability to reduce the complicated to the simple have immense power to facilitate change. Achievers realize that good communication facilitates quality change by enabling the entire organization to know why the change is needed, by identifying individual responsibilities as well as goals and time frames.

Those who aren't afraid to share information, who use language in a clear, concise manner, and intently listen to feedback have a talent few possess. It is a short leap from being a good communicator to being an achiever.

Without knowing the force of words, it is impossible to know men.

— Confucius —

A·C·H·I·E·V·E·R·S

"*Well timed silence hath more eloquence than speech.*"
— *Martin Tupper* —

"*A pen is certainly an excellent instrument to fix a man's attention and to influence his ambition.*"
— *John Adams* —

"*But in science the credit goes to the man who convinces the world, not to the man who the idea first occurs.*"
— *Sir Francis Darwin* —

"*The monuments of wit survive the monuments of power.*"
— *Francis Bacon* —

"*No one means all he says, and yet very few say all they mean, for words are slippery and thought is vicious.*"
— *Franklin Pierce Adams* —

A·C·H·I·E·V·E·R·S

" *Reading maketh a full man; conference a ready man; and writing an exact man.*"
— Francis Bacon —

" *The first function of the executive is to develop and maintain a system of communication.*"
— Chester Bernard —

" *The worse the news, the more effort should go into communicating it.*"
— Andrew S. Grove —
CEO, Intel Corp.

" *Too often the strong, silent man is silent because he does not know what to say.*"
— Winston Churchill —

" *Words are what hold a society together.*"
— Stuart Chase —

A·C·H·I·E·V·E·R·S

"How well we communicate is determined not by how well we say things but by how well we are understood."
— Andrew S. Grove —
CEO, Intel Corp.

"The hearing ear is always found close to the speaking tongue."
— Ralph Waldo Emerson —

"The world is shrinking, because the world is communicating."
— Ameritech —

"Words fly, writings remain."
— Latin Proverb —

"Words once spoken can never be recalled."
— Horace —
65-8 B.C.

A·C·H·I·E·V·E·R·S

"Success depends on three things: who says it, what he says, how he says it; and of these things, what he says is the least important."
— John, Viscount Morley of Blackburn (1917) —

"The finest eloquence is that which gets things done."
— David Lloyd George —
British Prime Minister

"Sometimes you have to be silent to be heard."
— Stanislaw J. Lec —

"Men are never so likely to settle a question rightly as when they discuss it freely."
— Thomas Babington Macaulay —

"Written reports stifle creativity."
— H. Ross Perot —
Founder EDS, Inc.
1992 Presidential Candidate

A·C·H·I·E·V·E·R·S

"He listens well who takes notes."
— Danté —

"The difference between the **almost** right word and the **right** word is really a large matter – it's the difference between the lightning bug and the lightning."
— Mark Twain —

"A lot of people are lonely because they build walls instead of bridges."
— Anonymous —

"Rudeness is the weak man's imitation of strength."
— Eric Hoffer —
1902-1983

"Good communication is as stimulating as black coffee, and just as hard to sleep after."
— Anne Morrow Lindbergh —

A·C·H·I·E·V·E·R·S

"*Effective people have the ability to boil down complex issues into concise, straight forward statements of what should be done.*"

— John Conway —

"*Communicate downward to subordinates with at least the same care and attention as you communicate upward to superiors.*"

— L.B. Belker —

"*There is genius in reducing the complicated to the simple.*"

— C.W. Ceran —

"*The finest expression of respect is not praise or status, but a willingness to talk openly to a person.*"

— Les Bittle —

"*Most of us, swimming against the tides of trouble the world knows nothing about, need only a bit of praise or encouragement — and we'll make the goal.*"

— Jerome P. Fleishman —

A·C·H·I·E·V·E·R·S

"The first rule of style is to have something to say. The second rule of style is to control yourself when, by chance, you have two things to say; say first one, then the other, not both at the same time."

— George Polya —

"Sandwich every bit of criticism between two heavy layers of praise."

— Mary Kay Ash —

"The right to be heard does not automatically include the right to be taken seriously."

— Hubert Humphrey —

"No man would listen to you talk if he didn't know it was his turn next."

— Ed Howe —

"My father gave me these hints on speech-making: Be sincere ... be brief ... be seated."

— James Roosevelt —
Son of President Franklin D. Roosevelt
Businessman and Politician

A·C·H·I·E·V·E·R·S

"Man does not live by words alone, despite the fact that sometimes he has to eat them."
— Adlai E. Stevenson —

"Once you get people laughing, they're listening and you can tell them almost anything."
— Herbert Gardner —

"Better to remain silent and be thought a fool than to speak out and remove all doubt."
— Abraham Lincoln —

"Rhetoric is the art of ruling the minds of men."
— Nolan Bushell —

"To communicate, put your thoughts in order; give them a purpose; use them to persuade, to instruct, to discover, to seduce."
— William Safire—

A·C·H·I·E·V·E·R·S

"Memos just don't move much."

"The super-salesman neither permits his subconscious mind to broadcast negative thoughts nor give expression to them through words, for the reason that he understands that like attracts like and negative suggestions attract negative actions and negative decisions from prospective buyers."
— Napoleon Hill —

"Whenever one has anything unpleasant to say, one should always be quite candid."
— Oscar Wilde —

"I like the way you always manage to state the obvious with a sense of real discovery."
— Gore Vidal —
American Writer

"Everything that can be thought at all can be thought clearly. Everything that can be said can be said clearly."
— Ludwig Wittgenstein —

$\mathcal{A}$·C·H·I·E·V·E·R·$\mathcal{S}$

$\mathcal{B}$y definition,

communication

means two-way

communication.

Insecure individuals

don't like it. Bosses

don't like it,

but leaders and

innovators do like it.

— Mark Sheperd —
Chairman
Texas Instruments

◆ ◆ ◆ ◆

$\mathcal{K}$ind words

can be short and

easy to speak,

but their echoes

are truly endless.

— Mother Teresa —

" $\mathcal{G}$ood listeners generally make more sales than good talkers. "
— B.C. Holwick —

" $\mathcal{G}$reat minds discuss ideas, average minds discuss events,
small minds discuss people. "
— Laurence J. Peter —

" $\mathcal{T}$he best communicators show respect. Respect … is appreciation
of the separateness of the other person, of the ways in which
he or she is unique. "

" $\mathcal{G}$arden variety, everyday passion is the stuff of excellence. "
— Tom Peters & Nancy Austin —

" $\mathcal{H}$aving a voice differs from having a say. "
— Max Depree—

A·C·H·I·E·V·E·R·S

"Tis the good reader that makes the good book; in every book he finds passages which seem to be confidences or asides hidden from all else and unmistakably meant for his ear; the profit of books is according to the sensibility of the reader; the profoundest thought or passion sleeps as in a mine, until it is discovered by an equal mind and heart."
— Ralph Waldo Emerson —

"Communication performs two functions: to educate and liberate."
— Max Depree —

"Say what you have to say and the first time you come to a sentence with a grammatical ending — sit down."
— Sir Winston Churchill—

"If you can't be funny, be interesting."
— Harold Ross —

"The phone is the great equalizer of the American productivity and service movement."
— Tom Peters —

A·C·H·I·E·V·E·R·S

People

change and forget

to tell each other.

— Lilian Hellman —
American Playwright
and Writer

◆ ◆ ◆ ◆

Think like a

wise man but

communicate in

the language of

the people.

— William Butler Yeats —

◆ ◆ ◆ ◆

I'll pay more for

a man's ability to

express himself than

for any other quality

he might possess.

— Charles Schwab —

"*If you want to persuade people, show the immediate relevance and value of what you're saying in terms of meeting their needs and desires ... Successful collaborative negotiation lies in finding out what the other side really wants and showing them a way to get it; while you get what you want.*"
— Herb Cohen —
You Can Negotiate Anything

"*Never argue; repeat your assertion.*"
— *Robert Owen* —

"*Use soft words and hard arguments.*"
— *English Proverb* —

"*Half the world is composed of people who have something to say and can't, and the other half who have nothing to say and keep on saying it.*"
— *Robert Frost* —

"*Many men know how to flatter, few men know how to praise.*"
— *Greek Proverb* —

A·C·H·I·E·V·E·R·S

"You can have brilliant ideas, but if you can't get them across, your ideas won't get you anywhere."
— *Lee Iacoca* —

"It takes an average person almost twice as long to understand a sentence that uses a negative approach than it does to understand a positive sentence."
— *John H. Reitmann* —
Psychiatrist

"If you can't get people to listen to you any other way, tell them it is confidential."
— *Farmer's Digest* —

"When it comes to body language, there are some who have better vocabularies than others."
— *Doug Larson* —

"The most important thing in communication is to hear what isn't being said."
— *Peter Drucker* —

Honesty

Achievers in today's society tend to be leaders; they are the people who are looked up to. Leaders today cannot shrink from their obligation to set a moral example.

Honesty is recognizing basic truths and then living them without altering them to service our own purposes. The best leaders "walk their talk." Sounds easy, but in practice, it is very difficult.

Technology has revolutionized the way business is executed, but it hasn't done away with the need for character or the ability to think. Honesty is the cornerstone of all achievement.

Honesty is rare and greatly treasured by a society starving for it. People yearn to interact with others without having to maintain all the defenses they have erected around themselves to ward off deceit. People want to trust and when they feel they can trust, a person or a company, they stick with them.

When they find an individual or organization with a great deal of integrity and honesty, loyalty is fashioned. And loyalty is a mighty force in industry today.

A·C·H·I·E·V·E·R·S

"A good reputation is more valuable than money."
— Publilius Syrus —

"Great men are they who see that the spiritual is stronger than any material force, that thoughts rule the world."
— Ralph Waldo Emerson —

"Put not your trust in money, but put your money in trust."
— Oliver Wendell Holmes —

"More people are flattered into virtue than bullied out of vice."
— Robert Smith Surtees —

"One must have a good memory to be able to keep the promises one makes."
— Friedrich Nietzsche —

A·C·H·I·E·V·E·R·S

The supreme quality for a leader is unquestionable integrity. Without it, no real success is possible, no matter whether it is on a section gang, a football field, in an army or in an office.

—Dwight D. Eisenhower—

The time is always right to do what is right.

—Martin Luther King, Jr.—

"Nothing astonishes men so much as common sense and plain dealing."
— *Ralph Waldo Emerson* —

"Beware, as long as you live, of judging people by appearances."

"When you walk your talk ... people listen."

"Fortunate indeed is the man who takes exactly the right measure of himself."
— *Peter Mere Lathan* —

A·C·H·I·E·V·E·R·S

"To be trusted is a greater compliment than to be loved."
— George MacDonald —

"The wise and moral man shines like a fire on a hilltop."
— The Pali Canon —

"An honest man's word is as good as his bond."
— Miguel de Cervantes —

"I believe that every right implies a responsibility; every opportunity, an obligation; every possession, a duty."
— John D. Rockefeller —

"Live in such a way that you would not be ashamed to sell your parrot to the town gossip."
— Will Rogers —
American Humorist

A·C·H·I·E·V·E·R·S

"Honesty is the best policy."
— Miguel de Cervantes —

"Resolved, never to do anything which I should be afraid to do
if it were the last hour of my life."
— Jonathan Edwards —

"Conscience is the inner voice which warns us somebody may
be looking."
— H.L. Mencken —
1949

"No man can climb beyond the limitations of his own character.
"
— Viscount Morley —

"The louder he talked of his honor, the faster we counted our
spoons."
— Ralph Waldo Emerson —

A·C·H·I·E·V·E·R·S

"Honest labor bears a lovely face."
— Thomas Decker —

"A man always has two reasons for what he does —
a good one, and the real one."
— Anonymous —

"Fool me once, shame on you. Fool me twice, shame on me."
— American Indian Expression —

"Never promise more than you can perform."
— Publilius Syrus —

"Start with what is right rather than what is acceptable."
— Peter Drucker —

A·C·H·I·E·V·E·R·S

A reputation for a thousand years may depend upon the conduct of a single moment.

— Ernest Bramah —

♦ ♦ ♦ ♦

Character is the ability to say NO when everyone except your conscience is screaming YES.

— Richie Harris —

"*Those who stand for nothing fall for anything.*"
— Alexander Hamilton —

"*A promise made is a debt unpaid.*"
— Robert W. Service —

"*How a man plays the game shows something of his character; how he loses shows all of it.*"
— Camden County, Georgia Tribune *—*

"*Truth is usually the best vindication against slander.*"
— Abraham Lincoln —

"*By constant self-discipline and self-control you can develop greatness of character.*"
— Grenville Kleiser—

A·C·H·I·E·V·E·R·S

"True courage is the knowledge of right and the determination to do it. False courage is a willingness to do what is wrong because others say it is right."
— Josh Billings —

"Strong convictions precede great actions."
— Unknown —

"In matters of principle, stand like a rock."
— Thomas Jefferson —

"Think about quality in terms of truth and integrity."
— Max Depree —

"Honesty is the cornerstone of all success, without which confidence and ability to perform shall cease to exist."
— Mary Kay Ash —

A·C·H·I·E·V·E·R·S

The competitive urge is a fine, wholesome direction of energy. But... the desire to win must be wedded to an idea, an ethical way of life. It must never become so strong that it dwarfs every other aspect of the game of life.

— Edward R. Murrow —

♦ ♦ ♦ ♦

He that lies down with the dogs will rise up with the fleas.

— Barber —
The Book of 1000
Proverbs, *1876*

"Few men have the virtue to withstand the highest bidder."
— George Washington —

"Truth is the only safe ground to stand upon."
— Elizabeth Cady Stanton —

"Many people don't actually lie; they merely present the truth in such a way that nobody recognizes it."

"Honesty means integrity in everything. Honesty means wholeness, completeness; it means truth in everything — in deed and in word."
— Orison Swett Marden —

"Real integrity stays in place whether the test is adversity or prosperity."
— Charles Swindoll —

A·C·H·I·E·V·E·R·S

"The naked truth is always better than the best dressed lie."
— Ann Landers —

"There can be ethical mobility as well as financial, and it can
go down as well as up."
— Margaret Halsey —

"Honor is like a rugged island without a shore;
once you have left it, you cannot return."
— Nicholas Boileau —

"Honesty is a question of right or wrong, not a matter of policy."

"You'll never get mixed up if you simply tell the truth.
Then you don't have to remember what you have said,
and you'll never forget what you have said."
— Sam Rayburn —

A·C·H·I·E·V·E·R·S

> *"A well-rounded character is square in all his dealings."*
> *— American Saying —*

> *"Live your life so that your autograph will be wanted instead of your fingerprints."*
> *— Howard Duckly —*

> *"To go against one's conscience is neither safe nor right. Here I stand. I cannot do otherwise."*
> *— Martin Luther —*
> *1483-1546*

> *"A man of words and not of deeds is like a garden full of weeds."*
> *— Anonymous —*

> *"Credibility is linked to the issues that are most important to people at the times they are deciding whom they will follow."*
> *— James Kouzes & Barry Posner—*

Honesty is the single most important factor having a direct bearing on the final success of an individual, a corporation, or a product.

— Ed McMahon —

A·C·H·I·E·V·E·R·S

"Self trust is the first secret of success."
— Ralph Waldo Emerson —

"No person was ever honored for what he received.
Honor has been the reward for what he gave."
— Calvin Coolidge —

"We often pray for purity, unselfishness, for the highest qualities
of character, and forget that these things cannot be given,
but must be earned."
— Lyman Abbott —

"Character is a diamond that scratches every other stone."
— Bartol —

"The credibility gap is so wide that our suspicions are confirmed
by any official denial."
— Laurence J. Peter —

Men occasionally stumble over the truth, but most of them pick themselves up and hurry off as if nothing had happened.

—Sir Winston Churchill—

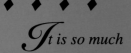

It is so much easier to do good than be good.

— B.C. Forbes —

"Dignity does not consist in possessing honors, but in deserving them."
— Aristotle —

"Aside from the strictly moral standpoint, honesty is – not only the best policy, but the only possible policy from the standpoint of business relations ... honesty begets honesty; trust, trust; and so on through the whole category of desirable practices that must govern and control the world's affairs."
— James F. Bell —

"Honesty is the first chapter in the book of wisdom."
— Thomas Jefferson —

"Truth or tact? You have to choose. Most times they are not compatible."
— Eddie Cantor —

"An ethical man is a Christian holding four aces."
— Mark Twain —

A·C·H·I·E·V·E·R·S

"The truth is more important than the facts."
— Frank Lloyd Wright —

"Dante once said that the hottest places in hell are reserved for those who in a period of moral crisis maintain their neutrality."
— John F. Kennedy —

"If you add to the truth, you subtract from it."
— The Talmud —

"Character is what you are in the dark."
— Dwight Moody —

"If you're going to do something tonight that you'll be sorry for tomorrow morning, sleep late."
— Henny Youngman —

A·C·H·I·E·V·E·R·S

"To be profoundly dishonest, a person must have one of two qualities: either he is unscrupulously ambitious, or he is unswervingly egocentric."
— Maya Angelou —

"Never give in, never never — in nothing great or small, large, or petty — never give in — except in convictions of honor and good sense."
— Tom Bradley —

"One falsehood spoils a thousand truths."
— Ashanti —

"Truth is patient and time is just."
— Frederick Douglass —
1876

"A person who is fundamentally honest doesn't need a code of ethics. The Ten Commandments and the Sermon on the Mount are all the ethical codes anybody needs."
— Harry Truman —

Keep in mind that the true measure of an individual is how he treats a person who can do him absolutely no good.

— Ann Landers —

A·C·H·I·E·V·E·R·S

"Not only can a man be honest and grow rich, but it is almost impossible for a man to grow rich until he is honest."

— J.J. Corn —

"Do not be too moral. You may cheat yourself out of much of life … Aim above morality. Be not simply good; be good for something."

— Henry David Thoreau —

"To live each day as though one's last, never flustered, never apathetic, never attitudinizing — here is the perfection of character."

— Marcus Aurelius —

"You cannot dream yourself into a character, you must hammer and forge yourself one."

— James A. Froude —

"Think of these things; whence you came, where you are going, and to whom you must account."

— Benjamin Franklin —

A·C·H·I·E·V·E·R·S

Intuitive

Achievers seem to possess an uncanny ability to anticipate the needs and trends of the marketplace. It is almost as if they possess extraordinary powers. Alas, there is no mystic source to their intuitive abilities. On the contrary, achievers are avid "students of the game" who have studied in perceptive detail the natures of the people, processes and products involved in their industry. When they make a decision based on these factors, it is an educated guess, not merely a hunch. This uncanny feel for the market may appear unrealistic to many, but it is the practical result of an individual who has listened to people, knows the processes and understands the market.

Perhaps the one factor that makes achievers appear uncommonly intuitive is that they are not afraid to be wrong. There is no telling how many good ideas go unfulfilled because of the fear of failure. Achievers realize that anticipating a need or trend will always include an element of risk. Their goal is to make the unknown as small as possible so that the intuitive momentum they have gained from knowing their people and their products will carry them.

A·C·H·I·E·V·E·R·S

"We heed no instincts but our own."
— Jean de La Fontaine —

"If the single man plants himself indomitable on his instincts, and there abide, the huge world will come round to him."
— Ralph Waldo Emerson —

"Never tell people how to do things. Tell them what to do and they will surprise you with their ingenuity."
— General George S. Patton, Jr. —

"You've got to take the initiative and play your game ... confidence makes the difference."
— Chris Evert —

"Three outstanding qualities make for success: judgment, industry, health. And the greatest of these is judgment."
— William Maxwell Aitken —

A·C·H·I·E·V·E·R·S

There are no logical paths to natural laws ... only intuition resting on sympathetic understanding of experience can reach them.

— Albert Einstein —

♦ ♦ ♦ ♦

A hunch is creativity trying to tell you something.

— Frank Capra —

"*Nothing in life is more exciting and rewarding than the sudden flash of insight that leaves you a changed person — not only changed, but for the better.*"
— Arthur Gordon —

"*Take calculated risks. That is quite different from being rash.*"
— George S. Patton —

"*Faith is the substance of things hoped for, the evidence of things not seen.*"
— Hebrews 11:1 —

"*What the inner voice says will not disappoint the hoping soul.*"
— Johann Christoph Friedrich Von Schiller —

"*The thing always happens that you really believe in; and the belief in a thing makes it happen.*"
— Frank Lloyd Wright—

A·C·H·I·E·V·E·R·S

"In any project the important factor is your belief. Without belief there can be no successful outcome."
— *William Jones* —

"Because of their agelong training in human relations – for that is what feminine intuition really is — women have a special contribution to make to any group enterprise."
— *Margaret Mead* —

"The best and most beautiful things in the world cannot be seen or even touched."
— *Helen Keller* —

"There is something that God has given me. It's an extra instinct for the game. Sometimes I can take the ball and no one can foresee any danger."
— *Pele* —

"As is our confidence, so is our capacity."
— *William Hazlitt* —

A·C·H·I·E·V·E·R·S

The last step to success frequently requires a daring intuitive leap...

— Roy Rowan —
The Intuitive Manager

♦ ♦ ♦ ♦

The most useful instinct is trained instinct.

— Henry Golightly —
Managing With Style

"*Ask people's advice, but decide for yourself.*"
— *Ukrainian Proverb* —

"*Keep focused on the substantiative issues. To make a decision means having to go through one door and closing all others.*"
— *Abraham Zalenznik* —

"*The biggest roadblock to creative decision making is not having the guts to follow a good hunch.*"
— *Roy Rowan* —
The Intuitive Manager

"*If you think you can, you can. And if you think you can't, you're right.*"
—*Mary Kay Ash* —

A·C·H·I·E·V·E·R·S

"Whenever you see a successful business, someone made a courageous decision."
— *Peter Drucker* —

"Never ignore a gut feeling: but never believe it's enough on its own."
— *Robert Heller* —
The Super Managers

"Progress in industry depends very largely on the enterprise of deep-thinking men, who are ahead of the times in their ideas."
— *Sir William Ellis* —

"Keeping a little ahead of conditions is one of the secrets of business."
— *Charles M. Schwab* —

"He who considers too much will perform little."
— *Schiller* —

A·C·H·I·E·V·E·R·S

"Instinct can be invaluable in running a business so long as it
is soundly based on reality."
— Henry Golightly —
Managing With Style

"All business proceeds on beliefs, or judgments of probabilities,
and not on certainties."
— Charles W. Eliot —

"Indecision is debilitating; it feeds upon itself … "
— H.A. Hopf —

"The percentage of mistakes in quick decisions is no greater than
in long drawn-out vacillations, and the effect of decisiveness
itself makes things go and creates confidence."
— Anne O'Hare McCormick —

"A business man's judgment is no better than his information."
— R.P. Lamont —

A·C·H·I·E·V·E·R·S

"What is wisdom? … I have often wondered, and I am not sure.
Understanding of life and men, I presume. It goes beyond mere
knowledge, as knowledge goes beyond information."
— Louis L'Amour —
Last of the Breed

"All our knowledge has its origins in our perceptions."
— Leonardo da Vinci —

"Faith means intense, usually confident, belief that is not based
on evidence sufficient to command assent from every
reasonable person."
— Walter Kaufmann —

"Conviction is a flame that must burn itself out — in trying an
idea or fighting for a chance to try it."
— Robert Townsend —

"There is no more miserable a human being than the one in
whom nothing is habitual but indecision."
— William James —

The best sales people in the world are the ones who have learned to use their sales instincts. They are the ones whose sense of intuition tells them what the customer needs, wants and likes, and then moves heaven and earth to give it to them.

— Kim Smithson —

"Everyone needs constant education and training. The more you keep yourself informed, the better your instincts and decision-making capabilities."

— Linda Conway —
Mentor Training Teacher

"In industry, it is never the industry leader who makes the big leap. On the contrary, it is the inventor or small guy who makes the big leap."

— Burton Klein —

"In sports, you have to go where you think the ball is going to be … not where it is."

— H.D. Leimann —

"Somehow I can't believe that there are any heights that can't be scaled by a man who knows the secret of making dreams come true. This special secret, it seems to me, can be summarized in four c's. They are curiosity, confidence, courage and constancy, and the greatest of these is confidence. When you believe in a thing, believe in it all the way, implicitly and unquestionably."

— Walt Disney —

"All growth is a leap in the dark, an intuitive guess backed by knowledge and experience."

— Henry Miller —

A·C·H·I·E·V·E·R·S

"An opportunity can only be grasped by those with the intuition and ability to see it."

— Howard Duckly —

"To understand others you should get behind their eyes and walk down their spine."

— Rod McKuen —

"There exist limitless opportunities in every industry. Where there is an open mind, there will always be a frontier."

— Charles F. Kettering —

"Self confidence, in itself, is of no value. It is useful only when put to work."

— Anonymous —

"I'm able to perceive what the issues are before they become issues."

— Stewart Alsop III —
The New York Times

People who don't take risks generally make about two big mistakes a year. People who do take risks generally make about two big mistakes a year.

— Peter Drucker —

♦ ♦ ♦ ♦

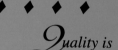*uality is all about the best way to do something, use your intuition to discover what the **best way** is.*

"*A flash of insight, the great idea, must be followed up with diligence, and a commitment to follow through ... the drudgery of grunt work ... or it becomes nothing more than a wishful dream.*"

— Howard Duckly —

"*Intelligent means a person who can see implications and draw conclusions.*"

— Babylonian Talmud, Hagiga —

"*Prediction is very difficult, especially about the future.*"

— Neils Bohr —

"*The prophet knows no more than ordinary man but he knows it earlier.*"

— Dagobert Runes —
A Book of Contemplation

"*If you don't look far enough ahead, you may not get good enough insights.*"

— Jason Yoon—
The Washington Post

A·C·H·I·E·V·E·R·S

"The difference between making the right decision and the wrong one lies not in what is obvious, but in what is subtle and often unseen."

— Ron Schultz—
Unconventional Quotes

"In most management problems there are too many possibilities to expect experience, judgment or intuition to provide good guesses, even with perfect information."

— Russell L. Ackoff —

"Put the policy manual back on the shelf when common sense points to a better way."

— Thomas Bonoma —
Harvard Business Review

"Where there is no knowledge there can be no insight, and where there is no insight there can be no knowledge."

— The Mishna, Sayings of the Fathers —

"A man should keep his little brain attic stocked with all the furniture that he is likely to use, and the rest he can put away in his mental library, where he can get it if he wants it."

— Sherlock Holmes —

A·C·H·I·E·V·E·R·S

The highest art of professional management requires the literal ability to smell a real fact from all the others.

— Harold Green, CEO —
IT & T

♦ ♦ ♦ ♦

Judgment is more than skill. It sets forth on intellectual seas beyond the shores of hard indisputable factual information.

— Kingman Brewster —

"*Follow your instincts. That is where true wisdom manifests itself.*"
— Oprah Winfrey —

"*The most successful business person is the one who holds on to the old just as long as it is good and grabs the new just as soon as it is better.*"

"*It is by logic we prove, but by intuition we discover.*"
— Henri Poincaré —

"*Business more than any other occupation is a continual calculation, an instinctive exercise in foresight.*"
— Henry Luce —

"*Creative people have much more confidence in their imaginative leaps, in their intuition.*"
— Laurel Cutler —

A·C·H·I·E·V·E·R·S

"The Eureka factor, that sudden, illuminating **I've found it** flash, has been referred to again and again by scientists attempting to describe the key element in their discovery process."

— Roy Rowan —
The Intuitive Manager

"Innovators use their intuition as a kind of sixth sense. It helps them access risks, read people, spot emerging patterns of change, and make complex decisions."

— Dr. Denis E. Waitley —
Winning The Innovation Game

"When possible make the decisions now, even if action is in the future. A reviewed decision usually is better than one reached at the last moment."

— William Given —

"Great minds must be ready not only to take the opportunities, but to make them."

— C.C. Colton —

"Your guess is as good as mine."

— American Saying —

ENTHUSIASM

Enthusiasm is the energy that drives success.
It's a **knock-down-drag-'em-out**, **never-say-die**,
can't-wait-'til-tomorrow attitude that simply overwhelms
failure. Most people admire this mindset in others not realizing
that they, too, possess the same capabilities. They incorrectly
relegate themselves to the sidelines of success
because of the fear of failure.

To be sure, achievers are not always successful in their efforts;
however, each of their efforts has a characteristic enthusiasm
about it that separates their effort from a mere attempt.
There is a vibrant, determined, all-or-nothing nature to each
venture they undertake. They radiate a contagious confidence
that can infect an entire department, team, or organization.
Their enthusiasm helps them and others to resist the
temptation to accept a standard, and instead
forges a new dynamic reality.

A·C·H·I·E·V·E·R·S

"*Fan the spark of possibility into the flame of achievement.*"
— *Unknown* —

"*Changing the inner attitude of your mind can change the outer aspect of your life.*"
— *Anonymous* —

"*Flaming enthusiasm, backed up by horse sense and persistence, is the quality that most frequently makes for success.*"
— *Dale Carnegie* —

"*My mother said to me 'If you become a soldier you'll be a general; if you become a monk you'll end up as the pope.' Instead I became a painter and wound up as Picasso.*"
— *Pablo Picasso* —

"*Every man is enthusiastic at times. One man has enthusiasm for thirty minutes, another has it for thirty days — but it is the man that has it for thirty years who makes a success in life.*"
— *The Catholic Layman* —

A·C·H·I·E·V·E·R·S

Enthusiasm is the electric current that keeps the engine of life going at top speed.

— W. Clement Stone —

♦ ♦ ♦ ♦

First make sure that what you aspire to accomplish is worth accomplishing, and then throw your whole vitality into it.

— B.C. Forbes —

"I rate enthusiasm even above professional skill."
— Sir Edward Appleton —

"An enthusiast may bore others, but he has never a dull moment himself."
— John Kieran —

"The world belongs to the energetic."
— Ralph Waldo Emerson —

"Strong lives are motivated by dynamic purposes."
— Kenneth Hildebrand —

"The real secret of success is enthusiasm. Yes, more than enthusiasm, I would say excitement. I like to see men get excited. When they get excited they make a success of their lives."
— Walter Chrysler —

A·C·H·I·E·V·E·R·S

"A man can succeed at almost anything for which he has unlimited enthusiasm."
— Charles Schwab —

"He who has no fire in himself cannot warm others."

"If you can't get enthusiastic about your work, it's time to get alarmed — something is wrong. Compete with yourself. Set your teeth and dive into the job of breaking your own record. No one keeps his enthusiasm automatically. Enthusiasm must be nourished with new actions, new aspirations, new efforts, new vision. It is one's own fault if his enthusiasm is gone; he has failed to feed it. If you want to turn your hours into minutes, renew your enthusiasm."
— Papyrus —
Old Egyptian Historical Papers

"Merit begets confidence; confidence begets enthusiasm; enthusiasm conquers the world."
— Walter Cottingham —

A·C·H·I·E·V·E·R·S

You only lose energy when life becomes dull in your mind. You don't have to be tired and bored. Get interested in something. Throw yourself into it with abandon.

—Norman Vincent Peale—

◆ ◆ ◆ ◆

Personal magnetism is a mixture of rugged honesty, pulsating energy, and self-organized intelligence.

— Arthur Dunn —

"*If a man is going to get ahead, if he is going to reach the top, he must be all wrapped up in what he is doing. He has to give his job not only his talent, but every bit of his enthusiasm and devotion.*"

— Samuel Goldwyn —

"*What hunger is in relation to food, zest is in relation to life.*"

— Bertrand Russell —

"*The most important thing is to love your sport. Never do it to please someone else – it has to be yours. That is all that will justify the hard work needed to achieve success. Compete against yourself, not others, for that is who is truly your best competition.*"

— Peggy Fleming Jenkins —

"*Nothing can stop the man with the right mental attitude from achieving his goal; nothing on earth can help the man with the wrong mental attitude.*"

— Thomas Jefferson —

"*Enthusiasm is a kind of faith that has been set afire.*"

— George Mathew Adams —

A·C·H·I·E·V·E·R·S

"Every production of genius must be the production of enthusiasm."

— *Benjamin Disraeli* —

"I prefer the folly of enthusiasm to the indifference of wisdom."

— *Anatole France* —

"Life is a romantic business. It is painting a picture, not doing a sum – but you have to make the romance, and it will come to the question of how much fire you have in your belly."

— *Oliver Wendell Holmes* —

"Our attitudes control our lives. Attitudes are a secret power working 24 hours a day, for good or bad. It is of paramount importance that we know how to harness and control this great force."

— *Charles Simmons* —

"You can't sweep other people off their feet, if you can't be swept off your own."

— *Clarence Day* —

A·C·H·I·E·V·E·R·S

Enthusiasm is the electric current that keeps the engine of life going at top speed. Enthusiasm is the very propeller of progress.

— B.C. Forbes —

♦ ♦ ♦ ♦

Apathy can be overcome by enthusiasm and enthusiasm can be aroused by two things: first, an idea which takes the imagination by storm; and second, a definite intelligible plan for carrying that idea into action.

— Arnold Toynbee —

"*Zeal without knowledge is fire without light.*"
— Thomas Fuller —

"*We act as though comfort and luxury were the chief requirements of life, when all that we need to make us really happy is something to be enthusiastic about.*"
— Charles Kingsley —

"*Nothing great in the world has ever been accomplished without passion.*"
— George Wilhelm Hegel —

"*Through zeal, knowledge is gotten, through lack of zeal, knowledge is lost.*"
— Buddha —

"*A wise man once said that enthusiasm is nothing but faith with a tin can tied to its tail.*"
— Anonymous —

A·C·H·I·E·V·E·R·S

"Enthusiasm is self-confidence in action!"
— Franklin Field —

"Our spirits grow gray before our hairs."
— Charles Lamb —

"If you aren't fired with enthusiasm, you will be fired with enthusiasm."
— Vincent Lombardi —

"The spirit of man is more important than mere physical strength, and the spiritual fiber of a nation than its wealth."
— Dwight D. Eisenhower —

"One of the strongest characteristics of genius is the power of lighting its own fire."
— John Foster —

A·C·H·I·E·V·E·R·S

Let enthusiasm radiate in your voice, your actions, your facial expressions, your personality, the words you use, and the thoughts you think!

—Ralph Waldo Emerson—

◆ ◆ ◆ ◆

Genuine enthusiasm comes when you feel you could touch a star without standing on tiptoe.

"What is the recipe for successful achievement? To my mind there are just four essential ingredients: Choose a career you love … Give it the best there is in you … Seize your opportunities … And be a member of the team. In no country but America, I believe, is it possible to fulfill all four of these requirements."
— Benjamin Fairless —

"Opposition inflames the enthusiast, never converts him."
— Schiller —

"Embrace change with enthusiasm and get the jump on everyone else!"
— Kim Smithson —

"A man is relieved and happy when he has put his heart into his work and done his best."
— Ralph Waldo Emerson —

"People who are unable to motivate themselves must be content with mediocrity, no matter how impressive their other talents."
— Andrew Carnegie —

A·C·H·I·E·V·E·R·S

"Enthusiasm reflects confidence, spreads good cheer, raises morale, inspires associates, arouses loyalty, and laughs at adversity … it is beyond price."
— Allan Cox —

"Confidence and enthusiasm are the greatest sales producers in any kind of economy."
— O.B. Smith —

"Motivation will almost always beat mere talent."
— Norman Augustine —

"Ambition should soar."
— Edmund Burke —

"The worst bankrupt is the man who has lost his enthusiasm. Let a man lose everything in the world but his enthusiasm and he will come through again to success."
— H.W. Arnold —

A·C·H·I·E·V·E·R·S

Like the chicken and the egg, enthusiasm and success seem to go together. We expect, however, that enthusiasm comes first. If you hope to succeed at anything in this world, polish up your enthusiasm and hang on to it.

— John Luther —

◆ ◆ ◆ ◆

Your face is a canvas … only you can paint the smile while others step back and admire it.

— Jenny Bumba —
Artist

"Each day you have to look into the mirror and say to yourself, 'I'm going to be the best I can no matter what it takes.'"
— Barbara Jordan —

"There is no ceiling on effort!"
— Henry Fruehauf —

"To make it to the top, you've got to want it with all your heart."
— Linda Wachman —

"Most people give up just when they're about to achieve success. They don't have enough enthusiasm. They quit on the one yard line. They give up at the last minute of the game one foot from a winning touchdown."
— H. Ross Perot —

"Nothing is as necessary for success as the single minded pursuit of an objective."
— Fredrick W. Smith —

A·C·H·I·E·V·E·R·S

"A winner is someone who sets his goals, commits himself to those goals, and then pursues his goals with all the enthusiasm he can muster."

"The people who succeed are the few who have the ambition and the willpower to develop themselves."
— Herbert Casson —

"Garden variety, everyday passion is the stuff of excellence."
— Tom Peters & Nancy Austin —

"Have confidence in your products and the house backing them, have enthusiasm for your job, call on your trade regularly and consistently, treat your trade courteously, and you will find that your customers will not have to be sold … they will be glad to buy."
— O.B. Smith —

"An enthusiastic team of talented individuals knows no boundaries."
— Anonymous —

A·C·H·I·E·V·E·R·S

"Don't bother about genius. Don't worry about being clever. Place your trust in hard work, enthusiasm, perseverance and determination."
— Sir Frederick Treves —

"A salesman, like the storage battery in your car, is constantly discharging energy. Unless he is recharged at frequent intervals he soon runs dry. He needs to be fired up!"
— R.H. Grant —

"A mighty flame followeth a tiny spark."
— Danté —

"Nothing splendid has ever been achieved except by those who dared believe that something inside them was superior to circumstance."
— Bruce Barton —

"Throw your heart over the fence and the rest will follow."
— Norman Vincent Peale —

A·C·H·I·E·V·E·R·S

"Everyone has noted the astonishing sources of energy that seem available to those who enjoy what they are doing or find meaning in what they are doing."
— Charles Garfield —

"Genius is initiative on fire."
— Holbrook Jackson —

"Nothing great or new can be done without enthusiasm. Enthusiasm is the fly-wheel which carries your saw through the knots in the log. A certain excessiveness seems a necessary element in all greatness."
— Dr. Harvey Cushing —

"The method of the enterprising is to plan with audacity, and execute with vigor; to sketch out a map of possibilities; and then to treat them as probabilities."
— Boveé —

"The basic foundation of excellence lies in personal pride, energy and enthusiasm."
— Dr. Dan Leimann —

ACHIEVERS

VISION

Vision is a startling moment of clarity — the ability to reduce the complicated to the simple. Vision needs passion for its start-up and patience for its endurance. Visionary people have the ability to articulate in detail a strategy of how to get from here to there. Successful vision has contingency plans for overcoming the multitude of naysayers. Achievers are those who latch on to an idea and have the mental map, determination and physical push to turn a thought or dream into reality.

Achievers are thinkers and dreamers. They have a natural inclination to dedicate spare moments to replay ideas and opportunities in their mind's eye. Men and women of achievement often see the whole as something greater than their part in it. They are able to coordinate the efforts of others and enlist their support, resulting in a well thought out plan. A complete vision inspires passionate belief and fuels action.

Achievers are simply those who understand there is little difference between obstacles and opportunities and have the vision to use both to their advantage.

A·C·H·I·E·V·E·R·S

"Thought is the original source."

— W. Clement Stone —

"If one is lucky, a solitary fantasy can totally transform one million realities."

— Maya Angelou —

"One can never consent to creep when one feels an impulse to soar."

— Helen Keller —

"We're all born under the same sky, but we don't all have the same horizon."

— Konrad Adenauer —

A·C·H·I·E·V·E·R·S

Vision without action is merely a dream. Action without vision just passes the time. Vision with action can change the world.

— Joel Arthur Barker —

◆ ◆ ◆ ◆

Good business leaders create a vision, articulate the vision, passionately own the vision, and relentlessly drive it to completion.

— Jack Welch —

"Your old men shall dream dreams, your young men shall see visions."

— Old Testament —
Joel 2:28

"Climb high; climb far; your goal the sky; your aim the star."
— *Inscription on Hopkins Memorial Steps, Williams College* —

"Hold fast to dreams, for if dreams die, life is a broken-winged bird that cannot fly. Hold fast to dreams for when dreams go, life is a barren field frozen with snow."
— *Langston Hughes* —

"Make no small plans for they have no power to stir your soul."

"The vitality of thought is in adventure. Ideas won't keep. Something must be done about them. When the idea is new, its custodians have fervor, live for it, and, if need be, die for it."

— *Alfred North Whitehead* —

A·C·H·I·E·V·E·R·S

"Cherish your visions and your dreams as they are the children of your soul; the blue prints of your ultimate achievements."
— Napoleon Hill —

"The only limits are, as always, those of vision."
— James Broughton —

"All men who have achieved great things have been dreamers."
— Orison Swett Marden —

"Begin with the end in mind is based on the principle that all things are created twice. There's a mental or first creation, and a physical or second creation to all things."
— Steven R. Covey —

"Discipline and focused awareness ... contributes to the act of creation."
— John Poppy —

Vision is a process that allows you to think ahead to where you want to be and what you want to be doing, and to create workable plans to lead you there.

— Fred Pryor —

♦ ♦ ♦ ♦

"A vision is not a vision unless it says yes to some ideas and no to others, inspires people and is a reason to get out of bed in the morning and come to work.

— Giford Pinchot —

"Vision is the art of seeing the invisible."
— Jonathan Swift —

"The three purposes of thinking: to solve problems, to create opportunities and to enrich the human condition."
— Abraham Lincoln —

"To dream anything you want to dream. That is the beauty of the human mind. To do anything you want to do. That is the strength of the human will. To trust yourself to test your limits. That is the courage to succeed."
— Bernard Edmonds —
American Writer

"We lift ourselves by our thoughts, we climb upon our vision of ourselves."
— Orison Swett Marden —

A·C·H·I·E·V·E·R·S

"Behind every successful venture, someone had a vision of how to make it work."

"Deep within man dwell those slumbering powers; powers that would astonish him, that he never dreamed of possessing; forces that would revolutionize his life if aroused and put into action."

— Orison Swett Marden —

"Dreams – there are no rules of architecture for a castle in the clouds."

— G.K. Chesterton —

"Where there is **no** vision, the people perish … "

— Proverbs, 29:18 —

"A strategy is trying to understand where you sit in today's world. Not where you were or where you hoped you would be … but where you are. It's trying to understand where you want to be. It's assessing the realistic chances of getting from here to there."

— John Welch, Jr. —
CEO, General Electric

A·C·H·I·E·V·E·R·S

The most pathetic

person in the world

is someone who

has sight but has

no vision.

— Helen Keller —

◆ ◆ ◆ ◆

Every man takes

the limits of his own

field of vision for the

limits of the world.

— Arthur Schopenhauer —
German Philosopher

"*Innovation is an attitude and a process of thinking strategically.*"
— Dr. Dan Leimann —

"*Treat your goals as guides, they should stretch and challenge*
you but not defeat you."
— David McNally —

"*Imagination is the highest kite one can fly.*"
— Lauren Bacall —

"*Don't part with your illusions. When they are gone, you may*
exist, but you have ceased to live."
— Mark Twain —

"*To have ideas is to gather flowers; to think is to weave*
them into garlands."
— Anne Sophie Swetchine —

A·C·H·I·E·V·E·R·S

"It's better to look where you're going than to see where
   you've been."

"All things that we conceive very clearly and very distinctly
   are true."

— René Descartes —

"Windows of opportunity exist for only a brief moment in time,
   you have to have vision in order to spot them, and take
   advantage of them."

— John Sculley —

"The greater thing in this world is not so much where we stand
   as in what direction we are going."

— Nolan Bushnell —

"Faith is the daring of the soul to go further than it can see."

A·C·H·I·E·V·E·R·S

If you can dream it

you can do it.

— Walt Disney —

♦ ♦ ♦ ♦

I skate where the

puck is going

to be, not where

it has been.

— Wayne Gretzky —

"*See things as you would have them be instead of as they are.*"
— Robert Collier —

"*The world of tomorrow belongs to the person who has the vision today.*"
— Robert Schuller —

"*A #2 pencil and a dream can take you anywhere.*"
— Joyce A. Myers —

"*A vision is articulated clearly and forcefully on every occasion. You can't blow an uncertain trumpet.*"
— Father Theodore Hesburgh —

"*If you really want something, you can figure out how to make it happen.*"
— Cher —

A·C·H·I·E·V·E·R·S

"*Efforts and courage are not enough without purpose and direction.*"
— John F. Kennedy —

"*A leader has the vision and conviction that a dream can be achieved. He inspires the power and energy to get it done.*"
— Ralph Lauren —
Chairman, Polo/Ralph Lauren Corporation

"*Business is like war in one respect. If it's grand strategy is correct, any number of tactical errors can be made and yet the enterprise proves successful.*"
— General Robert E. Wood —
President, Sears, Roebuck & Co.

"*A good goal is within your reach but just out of your grasp.*"
— Anonymous —

"*Man's mind, stretched to a new idea, never goes back to its original dimensions.*"
— Oliver Wendell Holmes —

A·C·H·I·E·V·E·R·S

"There is one thing stronger than all the armies in the world:
an idea whose time has come."
— Victor Hugo —

"All great deeds and all great thoughts have a ridiculous
beginning. Great works are often born on a street corner
or in a restaurant's revolving door."
— Albert Camus —

"Nothing pains some people more than having to think."
— Martin Luther King, Jr. —

"Necessity can set me helpless on my back, but she cannot keep
me there; nor can four walls limit my vision."
— Margaret Fairless Barber —

"The man who radiates good cheer, who makes life happier
wherever he meets it, is always a man of vision and faith."
— Ella Wheeler Wilcox —

A·C·H·I·E·V·E·R·S

" You must scale the mountain if you would view the plain."
— Chinese Proverb —

" A task without a vision is drudgery. A vision without a task
is a dream. A task with a vision is victory."

" Not through height does one see the moon."
— AFRICA —

" An idea, to be suggestive, must come to the individual with
the force of a revelation."
— William James —

" It's hard for young players to see the big picture. They just see
three or four years down the road."
— Kareem Abdul Jabbar—

A·C·H·I·E·V·E·R·S

" *I always had something to shoot for each year:
to jump one inch farther.*"
— Jackie Joyner Kersee —

" *The horizon is limitless to those who can see beyond the
obvious ... to those with vision.*"

" *Opportunities abound for men and women of vision, who when
they see a good idea, pick it up and are able to run with it.*"
— Kim Smithson —

" *Objectives are not fate; they are direction. They are not
commands; they are commitments. They do not determine
the future; they are means to mobilize the resources and
energies of the business for the making of the future.*"
— Peter F. Drucker —
People and Performance

" *People don't plan to fail – they fail to plan.*"
— William Siegal —

A·C·H·I·E·V·E·R·S

"*Leadership is the capacity to translate vision into reality.*"
— Warren Bennis —
President, University of Cincinnati

"*You see things and say, Why? But I dream things that never were; and I say. 'Why not?'*"
— George Bernard Shaw —

"*When a vision begins to form everything changes ... *"
— Jeane Dixon —

"*It is great to have creative zest. Have a sense of wonder and curiosity about the world. Have the boundless energy to explore, adventure and experiment with new ideas.*"
— Wilfred Peterson —

A·C·H·I·E·V·E·R·S

"Go as far as you can see and when you get there,
you will always be able to see further."
— Zig Ziglar —

"A good vision has an open mind about how to accomplish it."
— Anonymous —

"If you don't know where you're going, any path will take
you there."

— Sioux Proverb —

"The only limits to our realization of tomorrow will be our
doubts of today. Let us move forward with strong and
active faith."
— Franklin D. Roosevelt —

"Dreams are ... illustrations from the book your soul is
writing about."
— Marsha Norman —

A·C·H·I·E·V·E·R·S

"The key to innovation is collective creative effort. The key to creative effort is to collect a variety of ideas from a diverse group of people."

"Some things have to be believed to be seen."
— Ralph Hodgson —

"One ought to see everything that one has a chance of seeing; because in life not many have one chance and none has two."
— Sard Harker —

"The critical ingredient is getting off your butt and doing something. It's as simple as that. A lot of people have ideas, but there are few who decide to do something about them now. Not tomorrow. Not next week. But today. The true entrepreneur is a doer, not a dreamer."
— Nolan Bushell —

"Dreams — there are no rules of architecture for a castle in the clouds."
— G.K. Chesterton —

"To get where you want to go, you can't only do what you want to do."
— Peter Abrahams —

EXTRA EFFORT

Dedication and commitment, when exercised and developed at a young age, can command attitudes throughout a lifetime, not only in sport but in any given undertaking.

— Jerry Coleman —
Major League Manager

Achievers possess more energy than most people. Their seemingly endless energy reserves allow them to generate effort beyond the normal. The truth is, they don't have any special physical capability that gives them an unfair advantage. Instead, they have an advantageous mindset: do whatever it takes to get the job done well. They give each assigned task the effort it requires to be done well. To many people this appears like extra effort; although, to an achiever, it is only doing what is necessary. This start-to-finish, get-it-right attitude is common to all achievers. This special ingredient in their characters enables them to overcome barriers, meet or surpass deadlines, and obtain results.

Extra effort is a scarce commodity. Those who give everything they have … and then some, set industry standards and exceed beyond all expectations.

A·C·H·I·E·V·E·R·S

"Who can say what new horizons lie before us if we can but maintain the initiative and develop the imagination to penetrate them."

— Alfred P. Sloan, Jr. —

"Don't be misled into believing that somehow the world owes you a living."

— David Sarnoff —

"The big salaries in business go to those who have what it takes to get things done."

— J.C. Aspley —

"It's not half as important to burn the midnight oil as it is to be awake in the daytime."

— E.W. Elmore —

"It's amazing what ordinary people can do if they set out without preconceived notions."

— Charles F. Kettering —

A·C·H·I·E·V·E·R·S

There's no ceiling on effort.

— Harvey C. Fruehauf —

♦ ♦ ♦ ♦

Nothing worthwhile comes easily. Half effort does not produce half results. It produces no results. Work, continuous work and hard work, is the only way to accomplish results that last.

— Hamilton Holt —

"Big shots are the only little shots who keep on shooting."
— Christopher Morley —

"Most of life is routine — dull and grubby, but routine is the momentum that keeps a man going."
— Ben Nicholas—

"Poverty is uncomfortable; but nine times out of ten the best thing that can happen to a young man is to be tossed over-board and compelled to sink or swim."
— James A. Garfield —

"Excellence in any art or profession is attained only by hard and persistent work."
— Sir Theodore Martin —

"A man is relieved and happy when he had put his heart into his work and done his best."
— Ralph Waldo Emerson —

A·C·H·I·E·V·E·R·S

"The man who works for the gold in the job rather than for the
money in the pay envelope, is the fellow who gets on."
— *Joseph French Johnson* —

"Parties who want milk should not seat themselves on a stool
in the middle of a field in hope that the cow will back
up to them."
— *Elbert Hubbard* —

"Don't bother about genius. Don't worry about being clever.
Trust to hard work, perseverance and determination."
— *Sir Frederick Treves* —

"All philosophy lies in two words, sustain and abstain."
— *Epictetus* —

"No one ever attains eminent success by simply doing what is
required of him; it is the amount and excellence of what is over
and above the required, that determines the greatness of
ultimate distinction."
— *Charles Kendall Adams* —

In all human affairs there are efforts, and there are results, and the strength of the effort is the measure of the result.

—William Edward Hickson—

Winning isn't everything — but making the effort to win is.

— Vincent Lombardi —

"A barking dog is often more useful than a sleeping lion."
— Washington Irving —

"A fellow doesn't last long on what he has done. He's got to keep on delivering as he goes along."
— Carl Hubbell —

"Slow and steady wins the race."
— Aesop —

"The world is moving so fast these days that the man who says it can't be done is generally interrupted by someone doing it."
— Harry Emerson Fosdick —

"Don't wait for your ship to come in; swim out to it."
— Anonymous —

A·C·H·I·E·V·E·R·S

"You can be an ordinary athlete by getting away with less than your best. But if you want to be one of the greats, you have to give it all you've got — your everything."
— *Duke Kahanamoku* —

"Given willpower, he who has a firm resolve molds the world to himself."
— *Johann Wolfgang von Goethe* —

"If at first you don't succeed, try, try again."
— *William Edward Hickson* —

"Still achieving, still pursuing, learn to labor and to wait."
— *Henry Wadsworth Longfellow* —

"You may be disappointed if you fail, but you are doomed if you don't try."
— *Beverly Sills* —

The man who can drive himself further once the effort gets painful is the man who will win.

— Roger Bannister —

Always do more than is required of you.

— George S. Patton —

"I'm a firm believer that people only do their best at things they truly enjoy. It's difficult to excel at something you don't enjoy."
— Jack Nicklaus —

"There is no poverty that can overtake diligence."
— Japanese Proverb —

"You've got to love what you're doing. If you love it, you can overcome any handicap or the soreness or all the aches and pains, and continue to play for a long, long time."
— Gordie Howe —

"It's not whether you get knocked down, it's whether you get up."
— Vincent Lombardi —

"You never really lose until you stop trying."
— Mike Ditka —

A·C·H·I·E·V·E·R·S

"*If you consistently do your best, the worst won't happen.*"
— *B.C. Forbes* —

"*Satisfaction lies in the effort, not in the attainment.*"
— *Mohandas Gandhi* —

"*The harder you work, the luckier you get.*"
— *Gary Player* —

"*It doesn't matter if you're on the right track. If you're not moving fast enough, you'll still get run over.*"
— *Anonymous* —

"*Forty thousand wishes won't fill your bucket with fishes.*"
— *Fisherman's Saying* —

A·C·H·I·E·V·E·R·S

Achievers give more than they get. They operate without a scorecard. Their enthusiasm and effort propel them forward and ... over time they become the leaders to look up to.

— Kim Smithson —

◆ ◆ ◆ ◆

Elbow grease is the best polish.

— English Proverb —

"Genius is initiative on fire."
— Holbrook Jackson —

"Achievement-motivated people are not gamblers. They prefer to work on a problem rather than leave the outcome to chance."
— Paul Herset & Kenneth Blanchard —

"When the going gets tough, the tough get going."
— Anonymous —

"Effort is only effort when it begins to hurt."
— Jose Ortega Gasset —

"I swing big, with everything I've got. I hit big or I miss big. I like to live as big as I can."
— Babe Ruth —

A·C·H·I·E·V·E·R·S

"If you don't invest very much, then defeat doesn't hurt very much, and winning isn't very exciting."
— Dick Vermeil —

"Commitment is the willingness to do whatever it takes to get what you want. A true commitment is a heartfelt promise to yourself from which you will not back down. Many people have dreams and many have good intentions but few are willing to make the commitment for their attainment."
— David McNally —
Even Eagles Need A Push

"Those persons who want by the yard and try by the inch need to be kicked by the foot."
— W. Willard Wirtz —

"Effort is a commitment to seeing a task through to the end ... not just until you get tired of it."
— Howard Cato —

"Initiative is the active component of hope."
— Dr. Dan Leimann —

A·C·H·I·E·V·E·R·S

Despite the success cult, men are most deeply moved not by the reaching of the goal but by the grandness of effort involved in getting there — or failing to get there.

— Max Lerner —

◆ ◆ ◆ ◆

What is absolutely indispensible is strict follow-through, effort and stick-to-itiveness.

— Olga Korbut —

"*The heights by great mean reached and kept were not attained by sudden flight, but they while their companions slept, were toiling upward in the night.*"
— Henry Wadsworth Longfellow —

"*By patience and hard work, we brought order out of chaos, just as will be true of any problem if we stick to it with patience and wisdom and earnest effort.*"
— Booker T. Washington —

"*Let us not try to be the best or worse of others, but let us make the effort to be the best of ourselves.*"
— Marcus Garvey —

"*Nothing good comes in life or athletics unless a lot of hard work has preceded the effort. Only temporary success is achieved by taking short cuts.*"
— Roger Staubach —

"*I can't imagine a person becoming a success who doesn't give this game of life everything he's got.*"
— Walter Cronkite —

A·C·H·I·E·V·E·R·S

"Even when I went to the playground, I never picked the best players. I picked the guys with less talent, but who were willing to work hard ... and put in the effort, who had the desire to be great."

— Earvin "Magic" Johnson —
NBA Guard turned coach

"Every worthwhile accomplishment, big or little, has its stages of drudgery and triumph; a beginning, a struggle and a victory."

— Unknown —

"Unless you are willing to drench yourself in your work beyond the capacity of the average man, you are just not cut out for positions at the top."

— J.C. Penney —

"Luck is a dividend of sweat. The more you sweat the luckier you get."

— Ray Kroc —
Founder of McDonald's Corporation

"The quality of your work will have a great deal to do with the quality of your life."

— Anonymous —

A·C·H·I·E·V·E·R·S

"The price of success is hard work, dedication to the job at hand, and the determination that whether we win or lose, we have applied the best of ourselves to the task at hand."
— Vincent Lombardi —

"Instead of waiting for change to do something to you, you must take the effort to do something with it. This is how innovators win."
— Denis Waitley —

"If hard work is the key to success, most people would rather pick the lock."
— Claude McDonald —

"Nothing splendid has ever been achieved except by those who dared believe that something inside of them was superior to circumstance."
— Bruce Barton —

"Hit the ball over the fence and you can take your time going around the bases."
— John Rayser —

A·C·H·I·E·V·E·R·S

"The Golden Rule is of no use to you whatsoever unless you
   realize that it is your move."
                    — Dr. Frank Crane—

"The wayside of business is full of brilliant men who started out
   with a spurt, and lacked the stamina to finish. Their places were
   taken by patient and unshowy plodders who never knew when
   to quit."
                    — J.R. Todd —

"A professional is one who does his best work when he feels
   the least like working."
                    — Frank Lloyd Wright —

"The worse the news, the more effort should go into
   communicating it."
                    — Andrew S. Grove —

"Anybody can do just about anything with himself that he really
   wants to and makes up his mind to do. We are capable of greater
   things than we realize. How much one actually achieves depends
   largely on: 1. Desire 2. Faith 3. Persistent Effort 4. Ability.
   But if you are lacking the first three factors, your ability will
   not balance out the lack. So concentrate on the first three and
   the results will amaze you."
                    — Norman Vincent Peale —

A·C·H·I·E·V·E·R·S

REALISM

Achievers have often been described as daring chance takers who continually roll the dice until their lucky number comes up. Nothing could be more untrue, for achievers constantly keep their entrepreneurial pivot foot solidly placed on the basics of business as they creatively explore the limits of the marketplace. A firm grasp of human nature, supply and demand, and finances must never be lost. They are the barometers by which all innovation will be judged.

It should be noted that achievers do not necessarily limit themselves by a reality. On the contrary, they analyze the present reality of the marketplace in order to identify where it can be expanded. This makes reality a dynamic force rather than a limiting given. It makes reality a stepping stone rather than a headstone.

A·C·H·I·E·V·E·R·S

"Common sense is perhaps the most equally divided but surely
the most under-employed talent in the world."
— Christine Collange —

"What really matters is what you do with what you have."
—Shirley Lord —

"Having your feet on the floor and your head in the clouds is
not such a bad thing."
— Kim Smithson —

"Inspiration does not come like a bolt, nor is it kinetic, energetic
striving, but it comes into us slowly and quietly and all the time,
though we must regularly and every day give it a little chance
to start flowing."
— Brenda Ueland —

"Don't wait for your 'ship to come in' and feel angry and cheated
when it doesn't. Get going with something small."
— Irene Kassorla —

A·C·H·I·E·V·E·R·S

Don't be afraid of the space between your dreams and reality. If you can dream it, you can make it so.

— *Belva Davis* —

◆ ◆ ◆ ◆

You have to be realistic to be a good strategist, a good planner. Goals can't be set until reality has been focused ...

— *Patty Leimann* —

" *You rarely achieve more than you expect to get.* "
— *Carol Grosse* —

" *One characteristic of successful people from all walks of life is their internal accountability — they see themselves as responsible for gaining the excellence they seek and look inside for the strengths with which to achieve it.* "
— *Sidney Lecker, MD* —

" *Fixing your objective is like identifying the North Star — you sight your compass on it and then use it as the means of getting back on the track when you tend to stray.* "
— *Marshall Dimock* —
Author

" *Quality marks the search for an ideal after necessity has been satisfied and mere usefulness achieved.* "
— *Will A. Foster* —

" *Doers get to the top of the oak tree by climbing it. Dreamers sit on an acorn.* "
— *Anonymous* —

A·C·H·I·E·V·E·R·S

"To know what has to be done, then do it, comprises the whole philosophy of practical life."
— Sir William Osler—

"One of the big differences between the nonachiever and the achiever is that the latter has mastered the art of applying the obvious."
— Allan Cox —

"Professionalism is knowing how to do it, when to do it, and doing it."
— Frank Tyger —

"Character is determined by what you accomplish when the excitement is gone."
— Anonymous —

"A good sense of humor is essential to deal with the world's reality."
— Anonymous —

A·C·H·I·E·V·E·R·S

Today's reality can be changed for tomorrow. Within you right now is the power to do things you never dreamed possible. The power becomes available to you just as soon as you change your beliefs.

— Maxwell Maltz —

"An opportunity is reality seized!"
— Howard Duckly —

"Simplicity is a mark of greatness. 'To be simple is to be great,' wrote Emerson. Only little men pretend; big men are genuine, sincere and face reality."
— Wilfred Peterson —

"Triumph is just an 'umph' ahead of 'try'."
— Anonymous —

"Compared to what we ought to be, we are only half awake. We are making use of only a small part of our physical and mental resources. Stating the thing broadly, the human individual thus lives far within his limits. He possesses power of various sorts which he habitually fails to use."
— William James—

"Positive thinking is reacting positively to a negative situation."
— Bill Havens —

A·C·H·I·E·V·E·R·S

"What qualities ... characterize today's bizkids? ...
Self-confidence, ingenuity, an interest in finding practical
solutions to real problems — and a poet's belief that if the
first effort doesn't pay off, the world won't end."
— Peter Fuhrman —

"Neither a wise man nor a brave man lies down on the tracks
of history to wait for the train of the future to run over him."
— Dwight D. Eisenhower —

"The lure of the crisis is almost irresistible, because it demands
your immediate attention. But in retrospect, it is the high-priority
items that count."
— Mitchell J. Posner —

"Always behave like a duck — keep calm and unruffled on the
surface but paddle like the devil underneath."
— Jacob Braude —

"To develop and communicate a strategy, a unified sense of
direction to which all members of the organization can relate,
is probably the most important concept in business, and yet
the reality of it is frequently overlooked."
— Joel E. Ross and Michael J. Kami —

A·C·H·I·E·V·E·R·S

Change is reality.
And you can change
anything you want,
but you can't change
everything you want.

— John Rogers & —
Peter McWilliams

♦   ♦   ♦   ♦

An idealist
believes the short
run doesn't count.
A cynic believes the
long run doesn't
matter. A realist
believes that what
is done or left
undone in the short
run determines the
long run.

— Abraham Lincoln —

"If you do not think about the future, you cannot have one."
— John Galsworthy —

"The shortest distance between two points is under construction."
— Noelie Alito —

"Good plans shape good decisions. That's why good planning
helps to make elusive business dreams turn into reality."
— Lester Bittel —
The Nine Master Keys to Management

"Business is like riding a bicycle. Either you keep moving or
you fall down."
— John David Wright —

"We live in a fantasy world, a world of illusion.
The great task in life is to find reality."
— Iris Murdoch —

A·C·H·I·E·V·E·R·S

"You can never plan the future by the past."
— *Edmund Burke* —

"There's a mighty big difference between good, sound reasons
and reasons that sound good."
— *Burton Hillis* —

"Nothing is more terrible than activity without sight."
— *Thomas Carlyle* —

"I slept and dreamed that life was beauty;
I woke and found that life was duty."
— *Ellen Sturgis Hooper* —

"To achieve, you need thought. You have to know what you are
doing and that's real power."
— *Ayn Rand* —

A·C·H·I·E·V·E·R·S

"*Art is not a study of positive reality, it is seeking for ideal truth.*"

— George Sand —

"*The only thing that makes life possible is permanent, intolerable uncertainty; not knowing what comes next.*"

— Ursula K. LeGuin —

"*Work is reality. The achievers — that is, the movers, doers, and shakers — move up in the world because they face reality.*"

— Dr. Dan Leimann —

"*Even for those who face themselves, the most progressive will fight against other kinds of progress, for each of us is convinced that our way is the best way.*"

— Louis L'Amour —

"*Take responsibility for your dreams by turning them into reality.*"

— Anonymous —

A·C·H·I·E·V·E·R·S

"Nothing is as real as a dream. The world can change around you, but your dreams will not. Responsibilities need not erase it. Duties need not obscure it. Because the dream is within you, no one can take it away."

— Tom Clancy —

"If you have a dream, give it a chance to happen."

— Richard de Vos —

"Creativity is taking what is and making it something better."

— Anonymous —

"You are the same today that you are going to be five years from now except for two things: The people with whom you associate and the books you read."

— Charles "Tremendous" Jones —

"Achievement motivated people are not gamblers. They prefer to work on the reality of a problem rather than leave the outcome to chance."

— Paul Hersey —

A·C·H·I·E·V·E·R·S

There is no reality except the one contained within us. That is why so many people live such an unreal life. They take the images outside them for reality and never allow the world to assert itself.

— Hermann Hesse —

◆ ◆ ◆ ◆

The trouble with reason is that it becomes meaningless at the exact point where it refuses to act.

— Bernard DeVoto—

"*Real quality is free.*"
— *Philip Crosby* —

"*If you don't believe that goals can become reality … they will never happen.*"

"*A promise is a personal guarantee that will eventually become reality.*"
— *Austin Golub* —

"*The first law in advertising is to avoid reality … and cultivate the delightfully vague.*"
— *John Crosby—*

"*Reality is something to be discovered.*"
— *Peter Schrag* —

"No one can possibly achieve any real and lasting success or get rich in business by being a conformist content with reality."
— *J. Paul Getty* —

"Super sales people put the window dressing on reality."

"It was once rumored that fledging executives walked around their offices backwards so they wouldn't have to face the reality of an issue."
— *Fred Alken* —
Treadmill to Oblivion

"An ideal cannot wait for reality to prove its validity."
— *George Santayana* —
The Life to Reason

"The need for change bulldozed a road down the center of my mind."
—*Maya Angelou* —

A·C·H·I·E·V·E·R·S

"Reform must come from within, not from without. You cannot legislate for virtue."
— James Cardinal Gibbons —

"Like an ox-cart driver in monsoon season or the skipper of a grounded ship, one must sometimes go forward by going back."
—John Barth —

"Trends, like horses, are easier to ride in the direction they are already going."
— John Naisbitt —

"Reality is this ... only by his action can a man make himself and his life whole ... You are responsible for what you have done and the people whom you have influenced. In the end it is only the work that counts."
— Margaret Bourke-White —

"I made some studies, and reality is the leading cause of stress amongst those in touch with it. I can take it in small doses, but as a lifestyle I found it too confining."
— Jane Wagner —
The Search for Intelligent Life in the Universe

Each new season grows from the leftovers from the past. That is the essence of change, and change is the basic law of reality.

— Hal Borland —

A·C·H·I·E·V·E·R·S

"You have to accept whatever comes and the only important thing is that you meet it with the best you have to give."
— Eleanor Roosevelt —

"Some people have built-in filters that screen out the boos and amplify the hoorahs. Those are the people who never know when they're in trouble."
— Tommy Davis —

"Justice is the concept. Muscle is the reality."
— Linda Blanford —

"Discipline and focused awareness ... contribute to the act of productive creation."
— John Poppy —

"There is no real excellence in all this world which can be separated from right living."
— David Starr Jordan —

ACHIEVERS

SERVICE

The most successful individuals, and indeed the most successful organizations, are customer focused. An achiever in the business world quickly learns that the more he aligns his goal to match the needs of the customer, the more successful he will become. A passion to meet every single need and want of the customer for a given product or service is the hallmark of achieving people and organizations. This requires the ability to ask the right questions of the customer and to truly listen to the answers. The customer knows what he wants; an achiever finds out what it is.

In today's marketplace, there is keen competition to satisfy customers. Merely satisfying their needs only insures or maintains a given position of marketshare. The ultimate in customer satisfaction is to anticipate the customers' desires. Correct anticipation of a customer need can expand a marketshare, or in some cases, create an entire new market. Customer satisfaction is the bottom line in today's business world. Without question, achievers recognize that and make the customer their focus.

A·C·H·I·E·V·E·R·S

"The art of courtesy is the practice of the Golden Rule in little things."

— Wilfred Peterson —

"Life is not so short but that there is always time enough for courtesy."

— Ralph Waldo Emerson —

"Recognize the universal power of a smile; for a sincere smile is courtesy in every language."

— Wilfred Peterson —

"The sign brings customers."

— La Fontaine —

"Nothing is ever lost by courtesy. It is the cheapest of pleasures, costs nothing, and conveys much. It pleases him who gives and receives and thus like mercy, is twice blessed."

— Erastus Wiman —

A·C·H·I·E·V·E·R·S

" There is only one boss. The customer. And he can fire everybody in the company from the chairman on down, simply by spending his money somewhere else."
— Sam Walton —

" True service is courtesy even to those who are discourteous. It is striving to avoid a reaction or irritation in spite of the most severe provocation."
— Wilfred Peterson —

" Today's to-do list: satisfy a customer, satisfy a customer, satisfy another customer."
— Sign in the back room of a diner —

" Extra effort is what service is all about."
— Anonymous —

" There are just two ways of spreading light: to be the candle or the mirror that reflects it."
— Edith Wharton —

A·C·H·I·E·V·E·R·S

"Manners are a sensitive awareness of the feelings of others.
If you have that awareness, you have good manners …
no matter what fork you use."
— Emily Post —

"There is no happiness in having or in getting, but only in giving."
— Henry Drummond —

"To look up and not down, to look forward and not back,
to look out and not in, and to lend a hand."
— Edward Everett Hale —

"Always give people more than they expect to get."
— Nelson Boswell —

"Consumers are statistics. Customers are people."
— Stanley Marcus —

A·C·H·I·E·V·E·R·S

"Use your good judgment in all situations."
— Contents of the entire Nordstrom Employee Manual —

"Nothing is ever gained by winning an argument and losing a customer."
— C.F. Norton —

"We cannot hold a torch to light another's path without brightening our own."
— Ben Sweetland —

"The simple virtues of willingness, readiness, alertness and courtesy will carry a man farther then mere smartness."
— Davidson —

"Small kindnesses, small courtesies, small considerations, habitually practiced in our social intercourse, give a greater charm to the character than the display of great talent and accomplishments."
— Kelty —

A·C·H·I·E·V·E·R·S

" If things are not going well with you, begin your effort at
correcting the situation by carefully examining the service
you are rendering, and especially the spirit in which you are
rendering it."

— Roger Babson —

" Good customer service creates bonds that last."

— Theodore Levitt —

" Your market has a free choice, and only by supplying what the
market wants, and not by your efforts to impose your
merchandise, will you get your maximum share of the
market's potential."

— Walter H. Lowy —

" Thrill customers with immediate responsiveness."

" There are two kinds of failures: The man who will do nothing
he is told, and the man who will do nothing else."

— Dr. Perle Thompson —

A·C·H·I·E·V·E·R·S

The personal touch is so rare a commodity today, it becomes a standout.

— Harvey Mackay —
Humanize Your
Selling Strategy

◆ ◆ ◆ ◆

Service is an attitude of gratitude to the customer.

— Kim Smithson —

"Service to a just cause rewards the worker with more real happiness and satisfaction than any other venture of life."
— Carrie Chapman Catt —

"Striving for excellence … as long as the effort is there … keeps customers coming back."
— Anonymous —

"You can't live a perfect day without doing something for someone who will never be able to repay you."
— John Wooden —

"Kind words can be short and easy to speak, but their echoes are truly endless."
— Frank Pareta —

"Success comes from good judgment. Good judgment comes from experience. Experience comes from bad judgment."
— Arthur Jones —

A·C·H·I·E·V·E·R·S

"*Effective listeners remember order dates and quality specifications. They are easier to talk with when there's a problem with a shipment. In short, effective listeners sell more customers ... and keep them longer.*"
— Harvey Mackay —
Humanize Your Selling Strategy

"*It's amazing how much people can get done if they don't care who gets the credit.*"
— Sandra Swinney —

"*Customer satisfaction can be secured with a service guarantee. Committing to error-free service can help force a company to provide it.*"
— Christopher W.L. Hart —

"*Don't open a shop unless you know how to smile.*"
— Jewish Proverb —

"*Service is what life is all about.*"
— Marian Wright Edelman —

A·C·H·I·E·V·E·R·S

"*No one ever attains very eminent success by simply doing what is required of him; it is the amount and excellence of what is over and above the required, that determines the greatest of ultimate distinction.*"
— *Charles Kendall Adams* —

"*Innovation is service-oriented — searching for answers to the unmet needs and wants of customers.*"
— *Abraham Lincoln* —

"*Do it right the first time, do it very right the second time.*"
— *Service Excellence* —

"*Service is putting the customer first and last and a smile in between.*"
— *Kim Smithson* —

"*A well run restaurant is like a winning baseball team. It makes the most of every crew member's talent and takes advantage of every split-second opportunity to speed up service.*"

— *Ray Kroc* —
Founder of McDonald's Corporation

A·C·H·I·E·V·E·R·S

"Quality products and quality service begin with quality thinking."
— Harold McAlindon —

"Everybody can be great, because anybody can serve."
— Martin Luther King, Jr. —

"From now on, any definition of a successful life must include serving others."
— George Bush —

"Don't worry about profits, worry about service."
— Thomas Watson, Sr. —

"When a customer enters my store, forget me. He is king."
— John Wanamaker —

A·C·H·I·E·V·E·R·S

"Focus on pleasing the customer ... even if it means totally revamping the way business is done."

— Anonymous —

"Quality in a service or product is not what you put into it. It is what the customer gets out or it."

— Peter Drucker —

"Treat the customer as an appreciating asset."

— Tom Peters —

"In the United States, you say the customer is always right. In Japan, we say the customer is God. There is a big difference."

— James Morgan —

"Serve and sell."

— Early IBM Slogan—

A·C·H·I·E·V·E·R·S

"*What do customers want? Why that's simple …
The best of everything … "*
— Karyn Conway —

"*The valuable person in any business is the individual who can
and will co-operate with others."*
— Elbert Hubbard —

"*It is a funny thing about life; if you refuse to accept anything
but the best, you very often get it."*
— Somerset Maugham —

"*I solemnly promise and declare that every customer that comes
within ten feet of me, I will smile, look them in the eye, and
greet them, so help me Sam."*
— Employee pledge, Wal-Mart discount stores —

"*If you give something worth paying for, they'll pay."*
— Tom Peters —

Too much of a good thing can be wonderful!

— Mae West —

♦ ♦ ♦ ♦

Rule #1: The customer is always right. Rule #2: If the customer is ever wrong, reread Rule #1.

— Stew Leonard —

"*If a man writes a better book, preaches a better sermon, or makes a better mousetrap than his neighbor, though he builds his house in the woods, the world will make a beaten path to his door.*"

— Ralph Waldo Emerson —

"*There is only one valid definition of business purpose: to create a customer.*"

— Peter Drucker —

"*The magic formula that successful businesses have discovered is to treat customers like guests and employees like people.*"

— Tom Peters —

"*Loyalty is the natural response to loyalty. For the most part, you get back what you put out.*"

— Bruce Hylan & Merle Yost —

"*Put the customer first, and do it from the start. If a customer has a good experience; two or three people are told. If a customer has a bad experience … ten people are told. The lesson here is simple: we need to treat customers like gold.*"

— Anonymous —

A·C·H·I·E·V·E·R·S

"Customers deserve the very best. It would be helpful if everyone
in business could, to paraphrase the American Indian
expression, walk a mile in their customer's moccasins."
— Norman Augustine —

"The fragrance always remains in the hand that gives the rose."
— Heda Bejar —

"The customer absolutely defines quality in every transaction.
Although perceived quality is the most subjective measure,
it is the key to successful customer retention."
— Mark Wakefield —

"A high quality and professional sales approach is a powerful
way to add value and differentiate yourself from your
competitors."
— Graham Roberts-Phelps —

"Be a source of information and knowledge for your customers,
by making yourself a valuable resource, customers will keep
coming back."

A·C·H·I·E·V·E·R·S

" *Two kinds of gratitude: The sudden kind we feel for what we take; the larger kind we feel for what we give.* "
— A.E. Robinson —

" *Whenever I may be tempted to slack up and let the business run for awhile on its own impetus, I picture my competitor sitting at a desk in his opposition house, thinking and thinking with the most devilish intensity and clearness, and I ask myself what I can do to be better prepared for his next brilliant move.* "
— H. Gordon Selfridge —

" *A gentle word, a kind look, a good-natured smile can work wonders and accomplish miracles.* "
— Hazlitt —

" *I do not believe you can do today's job with yesterday's methods and be in business tomorrow.* "
— Nelson Jackson —

" *Revere the customer. The customer defines the business. Like coming in out of the rain, customer reverence should be a conditional response. A basic instinct.* "
— Jim Schell —
Brass-Tacks Entrepreneur

A·C·H·I·E·V·E·R·S

"Customers cannot be satisfied until after they are not dissatisfied. Your first service priority should be to eliminate all the opportunities for dissatisfying customers, because they are what cause customers to leave. Then you can invest in satisfying and delighting them."

— James H. Donnely, Jr. —
Close To The Customer

"Pressed into service means pressed out of shape."

— Robert Frost —

"The noblest service comes from nameless hands, and the best servant does his work unseen."

— Oliver Wendall Holmes —

"We should render a service to a friend to bind him closer to us, and to an enemy in order to make a friend of him."

— Cleobulus —
6th Century B.C.

"To oblige persons often costs little and helps much."

— Baltasar Gracian —

$\mathcal{I} \cdot N \cdot D \cdot E \cdot X$

$\mathcal{I} \cdot N \cdot D \cdot E \cdot \mathcal{X}$

I·N·D·E·X

I · N · D · E · X

$\mathcal{I}$ · N · D · E · $\mathcal{X}$

B·I·O·G·R·A·P·H·I·E·S

Dr. Dan Leimann graduated from Loyola University School of Dentistry in 1972 and currently is Chief of Dental Services at Hines Veterans Hospital, where he has been on the quality steering committee since 1989. He has been a VA physicians' consultant and trainer for the TQI (Total Quality Improvement) program throughout the entire VA since the inception of the program. He is the chairman of strategic planning for field operations for VA dentistry. Dr. Leimann has given numerous speeches nationwide in both the private and government sector on TQI related topics.

Kimberly Smithson studied abroad at the University of East Anglia in Norwich England through 1986, and furthered her studies in communication at Bowling Green State University, in Bowling Green, Ohio. Ms. Smithson is the president of High Impact Products, Inc., a St. Charles, Illinois based company that she started in 1992. She is the co-author of numerous inspirational titles, including: America: Her People Pride and Progress, The Achievers, and Quality and Service Made Simple.

Jenny Bumba graduated from the Portfolio Center in Atlanta, Georgia in 1989. From 1991-1993 she worked at Celebrating Excellence, Inc., a motivational products company based in Lombard, Illinois, where she conceptualized and designed motivational wall decor, books, and greeting cards. Currently, Jenny works for Absolute Impressions, a division of Magnetrol International Inc., a manufacturer of level and flow instrumentation, based in Downers Grove, Illinois. Jenny credits her career in design and art to her grade school teacher, Debbie Thompson, for encouragement and guidance.